DAVID METZENTHEN

Illustrated by Michelle Ker

Published by
Sundance Publishing
P.O. Box 1326
234 Taylor Street
Littleton, MA 01460

First published 1999 as Supa Dazzlers by
Addison Wesley Longman Australia Pty Limited
95 Coventry Street
South Melbourne 3205 Australia
Exclusive United States Distribution: Sundance Publishing

ISBN 0-7608-4792-4

Printed in Canada

Contents

Chapter 1

Surfing saves me. I love it. It keeps me going, and that's the truth.

You see, at Blue Water Bay, surfing means a lot. If you can surf, you've got a life. And if you've got a life, you've got friends. And if you've got friends, you've pretty much got it made.

My name is Adrian Swift, and I'm boss of the wash. I rule the waves. I have water on my brain and sand between my toes. I can paddle all day and dream of surf all night. Unfortunately I'm not so great at math—and a few other subjects at school.

Nope, Adrian Swift is not great at math. Nor is he a demon speed-reader or a mighty writer. Nope, I'm a bit of a dud at all that stuff, but I get by—just!

Anyway, so here I am at school, bumbling along in class when Mr. Bilsen brings in a new guy. And this new guy's name is Lucky Phil. Well, actually it's just Phillip, but for some reason, all the Phillips I know are always called Lucky.

So Lucky Phil sits down and gets to work. He's reading and writing, and I'm stumbling and sighing. He's looking at the board, and I'm looking out the window. And when the bell rings, I head for home. And then I go to the beach.

I hit the water with a whack. I paddle way out past the breakers and sit looking backward. And when a set of waves comes through, I catch the best wave and lock into it like a thrill-seeking missile.

I take off, I make turns, I get air. In other words, brothers and sisters, I surf!

I get energy from the wave. I do the waltz on water. I rev up with salt spray and sea breeze. And when I've had enough, I sit on the beach and watch the waves curl and unfurl. And then I see Lucky Phil Dillon, the new guy.

Lucky Phil's no surfer—like, he's wearing school shoes on the beach. His hair is short and black. Mine is blonde and held in twenty tight, spiky plaits. The older surf guys call me Hedgehog. My friends call me Addy. The girls call me cute. I call out to Lucky Phil.

"Hey, Phil. What's happening, man?"

I don't mind new people. I'm a pretty easy-going sort of guy. Besides, I think Phil might be lost. No one would wear those clothes on the beach unless they were. Phil comes over.

"Hello," he says. "How are the waves?" He glances out to sea, then he looks at my beautiful new board.

"Great," I say. "Do you surf?"

He shakes his head. He's got a plain haircut and a serious face. He looks like my dentist!

"No, I come from the city," says Phil, and he looks back out to sea. "Belmore—there aren't any waves there."

I look out to sea, too. The swell has
dropped, and the water slops around like
dark blue soup. No more presents from the
sea gods. Time to head for home.

"You'll have to get a board, Phil," I say, and
stand up. "You can't surf without one, you
know."

Phillip smiles. "I'd sure like to learn. It looks pretty difficult, though."

"Phil," I say. "It's nothing compared to walking on the beach with those shoes on. Now that's *hard*—and it's against the law around here!"

Phillip grins. "I'm not used to the beach."

I grin at him. "You're kidding? Anyway, you'll learn. I'm Adrian." I pick up my board. "See you." I walk away up the path.

Imagine not being able to surf. Imagine living in the city. Imagine being called Phillip. I can't.

Chapter 2

Sea Gulls Just Aren't Cool

You learn a lot at the beach. Being a surfer isn't just about catching waves and impressing the girls. To be a good surfer you've got to know a lot about a lot.

I can tell you about wind, I can tell you about water—but I won't. What I will tell you about is sea gulls. Sea gulls only hang around with sea gulls. Sea gulls think they own the place. Sea gulls squawk and squabble. Sea gulls are brats basically—like some of my buddies, sometimes! And I'll tell you why. It all has to do with Lucky Phil.

Okay, so we all know Phil Dillon isn't all that cool. He can't surf or ride a sailboard—man, maybe he can't even swim, but so what? Give the guy a chance to settle in, I say . . . but that is not what is happening.

My pals are giving Lucky Phil the treatment. Mop-head and Marco-man don't like Phil's clothes, and they don't like Phil's haircut.

They don't like the way Phil talks, they don't like the way Phil walks. Man, they don't like Phil. They don't know him, but they don't like him.

Sea gulls, you see—my pals are sea gulls. And that's embarrassing because sea gulls just aren't cool.

I have spoken. And now I'm going surfing.

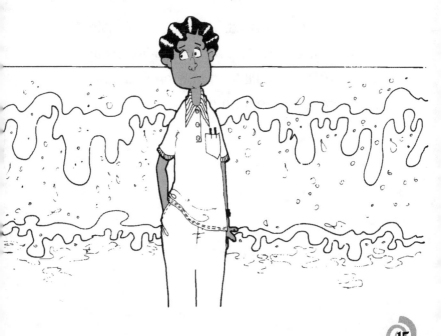

I surf. I catch waves—and the waves I catch set me free. Then I walk home with the sound of the sea in my head. And as I'm walking, I see Phil Dillon.

Lucky Phil's looking in the window of the Blue Water Bay surf shop. So I walk up and ask him what he's doing.

"Window shopping," he says. "I'm going to buy a board."

I check out the boards. I check out Phillip. I make a suggestion. "Phil," I say, "*try* before you buy, buddy. I'll lend you one." It's no problem, you see. I have six.

Suddenly Phillip kind of sags. For the past two weeks, he's been walking around like the world's bravest soldier—now he looks like a different kid. He looks like he might cry.

"*You'll* lend me one of your boards?" he asks. "*Me?*"

"Yeah, sure, Phil," I say. "No problem."

What I don't say is that *I'm* Adrian Swift, and Adrian Swift is *no* sea gull. I fly high, and I don't mind flying alone.

"I'll bring it to school," I tell him. "You can try it out tomorrow afternoon."

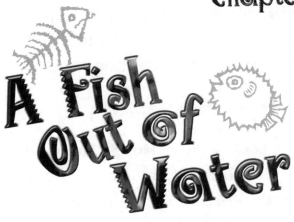

Chapter 3

A Fish Out of Water

I walk into math class with my surfboard. Mop-head and Marco-man laugh, but when I put it on Phil Dillon's desk, old Moppsy starts to squawk.

"What are you doing, Adrian? What are you doing, man? That guy's a *goose!*"

I sit down. "Maybe he is, Mopps," I say, "but at least he's not a sea gull."

I don't explain. Besides, sea gulls understand actions better than words. But as for math and whatever else is on the board . . . well, Adrian Swift doesn't understand that at all.

See? No one's perfect.

After school I surf with Moppsy and Marco-man. We're out pretty far from the beach, and Lucky Phil is right in front of us.

"He's not a bad swimmer," says Moppsy.

"Which is lucky," says Marco, "because he's doing a lot of it."

"I just hope," I say, "that he's taken off his school shoes."

I catch a wave. I cut and carve. I turn and burn. I'm in my element—water! And man, what can I say? It's a beautiful thing!

We sit on the beach and watch Phillip.

"Hopeless," says Moppsy, shaking his shaggy head.

"Useless," says Marco, pointing a stick.

"Beginner," I say. "Give the guy a break."

Mop-head looks at me from under his fringe of thick, black hair. "Ad, why do you like this Phil? He's a loser."

I watch Phil Dillon get smashed by a wave. "Well," I say, "I don't know if I do like him, really."

Marco jumps up and down. "Then *why'd* you lend him a board, Addy? Why? Why? *Why?*"

I don't exactly know why I did lend Phil a board. I just get the feeling that he's all right. He deserves a chance, at least.

"He wanted to try to surf," I tell Marco. "What's the problem with that?"

We watch Phil struggle up the beach. He drops the board on his foot.

"The problem *is*," says Marco-man, "that he's absolutely hopeless."

Well, Phil Dillon might not be *absolutely* hopeless, but I must admit he is like a fish out of water. And when he is in the water, he's nothing like a fish at all—which is bad luck for Phil, however you look at it!

Phil and I walk up through the dunes. There are huge black clouds far out to sea. Big waves will soon be coming. Marco and Moppsy are still on the beach.

"Keep the board for a while, Phil," I say. "No one learns to surf in a day."

He thanks me, and we stop to look at the water. It's gray like steel now. The waves have dropped . . . the calm before the storm.

Chapter 4

Aysha

I live among trees. Our house is nothing much to look at, but it's great to live in. It has a veranda and a long, dirt driveway. I can hear the waves through my bedroom window.

So there I am on Thursday afternoon, in my wet suit, looking in the mailbox, when a girl appears. She is small. Her eyes are dark, her hair is darker, and she's pretty—pretty cute, that is.

"Hello," she says, "I'm Phillip Dillon's sister. My name's Aysha, and you're Adrian, aren't you? The girls at school told me."

"Whatever you say," I say and grin. I like girls. I like this one already. I can tell she's smart. I can *see* she's beautiful!

She smiles, too. "Thanks for lending Phillip a surfboard. He says he's going to practice every day until he can catch a decent wave."

I nod. "Yeah, well, it takes a while."

Aysha smiles, then walks away. I go across the road to the beach. And when I get to the top of the path I see Phil out in the water. He falls off the board, he gets back on. Then he falls off again.

Well, that's okay. You'll never succeed if you give up, will you?

Chapter 5

Waiting, Waiting, Waiting

Mathematics equals confusion. That's what I think, anyway. Adrian Swift is not a numbers man, no sir.

When I look at a page of math problems, I feel sick. All those little black numbers and little black signs have beaten me before I've even started. I see total failure in my future. I close my book and dream of waves that have my name written on them in sunshine and bubbles.

After school I surf, and Phil struggles. I blast past him and into the beach. Then I stop to see how he's doing—and he's not doing very well. But he is doing better than he was the other day. I guess I'd better give him some more advice. So I yell at him to pick the smallest waves, not the biggest. This makes sense!

At home I watch the weather report on TV. It's my favorite show. I see the storm clouds are farther out to sea—where they are busy making waves. And that means, boys and girls, hold on to your hats, because soon there'll be more surf than you can shake a stick at. *Man*, I can't wait!

So, because I can't wait, I go down to the beach to see what I can see. But all that I can see is flat water . . . and Phil. "Phil!" I call out. "Give it a rest, man! Come back in a couple of days. There'll be waves then— monsters!"

I guess I've been thinking about surfing so much I forgot about the BIG MATH TEST. This megatest is in a few days . . . and so are the giant surf swells made by the storm out at sea. The only difference is, I can hardly wait for the waves—but I wouldn't mind waiting forever for the math test.

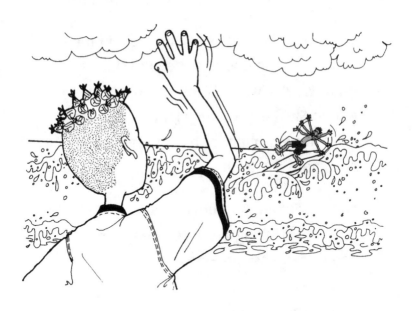

I've flunked math tests before. But this test is different. If I fail it, I'm going to be put in a special class . . . by myself. And I do not want to be in a special class by myself.

I do not want to be the only guy working with Ms. Radcliff because Ms. Radcliff only teaches the slowest kids. And Adrian *Swift* does not want to be known as Adrian *Slow*.

What would the guys say if I were in the *slow* class? What would the guys think? What would Aysha Dillon think? Look, Adrian Swift is no sea gull, but I sure don't want to be thought of as a goose, either. And that's the truth.

I have spoken. And now I'm going to go and do some thinking because I need a plan, and I need answers—now.

Bingo!

I have a plan, and this plan will give me *everything* I need. What I will do is simply sit very close to Phil—and "borrow" some of his work.

The guy's smart, and he's fast. And he would never suspect that I, Adrian Swift, might cheat. After all, Lucky Phil believes honest

Adrian Swift is the only good guy in the whole of Blue Water Bay.

I cheat on the math test. Not a lot, but enough to get me through—plus I grab a few extra answers to make it look like I've really improved . . . which I haven't.

Oh, well, as I've said before, no one's perfect.

After school the surf is building. It rises way out at sea and comes running in. The waves are big, but they're going to get bigger. And I catch every one I can get.

I surf hard. I put on a radical performance. And when I get back to the beach, all I can think of is the perfect ride—until I set eyes on Phil.

And then I think about how I cheated. And then I tell myself I don't care. Well, I don't much . . . do I?

Chapter 6

Walls of Water

I listen to the waves as I lie in bed. They thunder and boom, they roar and rage. I can imagine them charging at the beach. Tomorrow will be a surfing day no one will ever forget.

At school, all Moppsy, Marco, and I talk about are the waves. At school, all Moppsy, Marco, and I look at is the beach. And when the last bell rings, we head home for our boards and wet suits.

The beach has changed. It looks like it's under attack from the sea. The waves race in and break with the sound of bombs. Mopps, Marco-man, and I stand at the edge and look out. We have our boards. We can all surf—but we are certainly all scared.

"Man," says Mopps, "that is fierce."

"So," says Marco. "What do you guys think?"

I think we can handle it. It's big surf, but we've been in big surf before. Except that *this* surf is bigger than big. It's storm surf, powerful and wild. I study the water.

"I'll give it a go," I say. "I think I'll be OK."

Moppsy and Marco don't say anything, but when I walk into the water they are right behind me. I start to paddle. Over our heads the spray from the waves drifts like smoke.

Once we head out, we know we're in trouble. The surf knocks us back toward the beach, but we don't give up. Then there is a break between waves. And we make it out— right out.

"I've got to admit, Ad," says Marco, resting on his board, "I'm kind of worried about this."

"It's big," says Moppsy, watching the waves storm toward the shore. "Man, it is big."

"Yeah, it is," I say carefully. "Maybe you guys should just catch one in and call it a day."

Moppsy and Marco look at me and then at each other. The surf *ka-booms*.

"We'll see," says Moppsy. "Won't we, Marco-man?"

Marco-man nods. His face is pale. "Yeah," he says. "I guess we will."

Moppsy and Marco catch a wave in, but they don't paddle back out. That's okay, though. They're my friends. They've made an honest decision. They faced facts. I don't think they're weak. They figured out the truth, and they did the right thing.

I catch three waves, and each one pushes me along like a roaring steam train. Riding them is like falling off a cliff—then finding out you can fly. It's incredible! Then, suddenly, I decide to go in, too. Enough's enough. Don't disrespect the sea gods, that's what Adrian Swift says.

So I set about surfing in—and then I see Phil Dillon trying to paddle out. I watch Phil battling through the waves. He gets washed backward again and again. He gets rolled. He loses his board, but he keeps on trying.

Phil's crazy. He's not a strong enough swimmer or a good enough surfer for this. He should go in. In fact, he *has* to go back in, or he'll drown. And I'm the only one out here who can tell him. I take off on a wave with a message to deliver.

I crash-land beside Phil in the white water. He looks as if he's about to go under and not come back up again.

"Go in, Phil," I say. "Now!"

He gets back on his board.

"No, Adrian, I can handle it. I can."

He can't. I know he can't. He's kidding himself in a big way. And here comes another wave to prove it.

Water surges toward us. I push my board through it easily, but Phil gets carried yards backward. I paddle to him, shouting.

"Phil! We're going in! You can't handle it! Admit it, pal, or you'll drown!"

He stares at me. "I *can* handle it. I—" He sags onto his board. "You're right. I've had it."

I grab his arm and talk right into his face. "Just listen and everything'll be okay, all right? Listen to me, Phil! Are you listening?"

He nods, his eyes wide.

"Right," I say. "Turn around, and let the waves do the work. Just hang on. Like this." I show him how, and slowly we go in.

Moppsy, Marco, Phil, and I walk off the
beach. The waves crash behind us.

"Hey, guys," says Phil, and stops on the path.
"I was an idiot back there."

We stop.

"Yeah, you were," says Moppsy.

"I shouldn't have gone in," Phil says. "I was
kidding myself."

"Yep," says Marco, "that's true."

Well, at least Phil admits he was wrong,
which is a step in the right direction.
Setting off in the right direction is the
most important thing when you're trying
to get anywhere.

Chapter 7

Facing the Music

I'm going to turn myself in. I'm going to face the music. Sometimes you have to stop, think, and turn around to find the right direction. So I'm going to do just that. I'm on my way right now—to see Ms. Radcliff, math teacher to the nonstars.

Adrian Swift is now in a math class of one. I am going back to the beginning. I'm learning the basics. And it's not so bad. At least now I understand what's going on. At least now I've stopped trying to kid myself.

I've got to tell you—I like Ms. Radcliff. The first thing she did was to get me to multiply the number of fins on my surfboard by the number of plaits on my head. Now you're talking!

Chapter 8

#

The surf has dropped, and even Phil has been able to catch a wave. Moppsy and Marco-man have decided he's OK now and have let him become one of the surf crew.

I like Phil Dillon. Like, he's not a natural surfer, but he's a guy you can rely on. I like his sister, Aysha, too. But I will not let her become one of the guys. I like her exactly as she is. And I'm getting the vibe that she thinks I'm OK, too. Which is good, because we're going away together.

Let me explain. City people go to the beach for vacation, right? Right. So why shouldn't beach people go to the city? Right again. And that is what is happening. I'm taking off for town with Phil Dillon, his parents, and Aysha.

The Dillons still keep an apartment in Belmore for vacations. It's smack in the middle of the city on the fourteenth floor of a high-rise. Hey! Feels like there's a sky-high adventure coming on, if you ask me.

So ask me, and I'll tell you what happens— because if I'm going to town, I'm not going quietly. And remember, you'll always hear the truth from honest Adrian Swift . . . in the end, anyway.

I have spoken. And now I'm going surfing.

Catch you soon!

About the Author

David Metzenthen

David Metzenthen tries really hard to write books that most definitely could be true! He is interested in sailboarding, indoor rock climbing, fishing, the environment, and good books. He is married and has two children and a goldfish called George, who eats like a horse.

David likes to write stories that contain action, adventure, and ideas about life. He hopes that his stories and characters will find a place in your memory, as well as on your bookshelf.

About the Illustrator

Michelle Ker

Michelle Ker lives in a big, old rambling house with a dog, a cat, and some nosy neighbors who think she is odd and wonder what she does all day in that room under the house.

Michelle loves music and plays drums. She gets a lot of the ideas for how characters look from watching rock bands.

She does all kinds of drawings for all kinds of people, but she likes drawing for kids' books the best. The characters have more fun, do mischievous things, and have better hairdos than people in other kinds of books.